DARE TO
BE DIFFERENT,
DARE TO
BE CHRISTIAN

*CHARLES
COLSON*

VICTOR

BOOKS a division of SP Publications, Inc.

WHEATON, ILLINOIS 60187

Offices also in
Whitby, Ontario, Canada
Amersham-on-the-Hill, Bucks, England

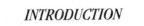

We live in a time that would seem to be marked by unprecedented spiritual resurgence: 96 percent of all Americans say they believe in God; 80 percent profess to be Christians.

Yet families are splitting apart in record numbers. Countless millions of unborn children have been murdered since 1973. And there are 100 times more burglaries in so-called "Christian" America than in so-called "pagan" Japan.

Why this paradox between profession and practice? Why is the faith of more than 50 million Americans who claim to be born again not making more of an impact on the moral values of our land?

The answer is what Dietrich Bonhoeffer, the German pastor martyred by the Nazis, labeled cheap grace: the perception that Christianity offers only a flood of blessings, the rights of the kingdom without responsibilities to the King. This easy believism fails to take biblical truth to heart and fails to act in obedience to the Scriptures. The result is a church which increasingly accommodates secular values. Not knowingly, of course, but simply by gradual acceptance of secular standards which have become comfortable.

We needn't fear a sinister conspiracy to impose atheism on our society. Though such forces may be at work, they will fail precisely because they are overt.

No, the real peril today comes from the subtle ways in which the mind of our culture is being gradually won over to secular values—in the media, in classrooms, and tragically, even in our church pews. This threat is all the more insidious because it is unseen. It is the cancer of compromise.

God is calling His people today to challenge secular values, measuring them in the light of biblical revelation. Will we cave in to a culture which in principle and practice denies Christ's lordship, or will we heed His call and stand for Him?

Doing so will put us in sharp conflict with much of what the world exalts, but that must be our witness. Two centuries ago, John Wesley wrote, "Making an open stand against all ungodliness and unrighteousness, which overspreads our land as a flood, is one of the noblest ways of confessing Christ in the face of His enemies."

I can think of no more timely challenge for the Christian church today.

DARE TO
BE DIFFERENT,
DARE TO
BE CHRISTIAN

America is a nation in transition, in the eye of a storm which pollster Daniel Yankelovich calls a "sweeping, irreversible cultural revolution . . . transforming the rules that once guided American life." Powerful forces are shaking our very substructure.

Like all revolutions, the most profound struggle is going on in *us.* We are desperately seeking certainty in the midst of confusion and hope in the face of disillusionment. Above all we are confounded by the maddening

contradictions which plague us.
Consider just these four illustrations:

- The boundless affluence considered to be the fulfillment of the American dream led to indifference and spiritually destructive materialism.

- The technology which promised to lead mankind to a new promised land now threatens to obliterate it in a giant mushroom cloud.

- The self-fulfillment spree of the '70s led not to the expected expansion of the human potential but to isolation, loneliness, and the death of community.

- The lofty visions of freedom and democracy which ennobled America's mission as a world power floundered in the rice paddies of a distant continent, raising unprecedented and unanswered moral questions.

Our dilemmas are compounded by a technology which dramatically telescopes history, accelerating the speed of cultural change. While it took early pioneers a full century on foot and hoof to hack their way across the wilderness of this continent, the jet age measures such distance in hours and seconds. So today's pilgrimage is that of a people being propelled through a wind tunnel, tumbling and falling helplessly, unable to gain secure footing long enough to catch their breath.

Jacques Ellul, the French lawyer-theologian, wrote: "Day after day the wind blows away the pages of our calendars, our newspapers, and our political regimes, and we glide along the stream of time without a judgment. . . . If we are able to live in this world . . . we need to rediscover the meanings of events and the spiritual framework which our contemporaries have lost." Precisely! We are a people wandering in a spiritual wilderness, searching frantically for our roots and crying out for an understanding of the context in which we live.

Deeper Issues

If you follow daily headlines you will quickly conclude that the dominant issues in American society are inflation and economic policy, or defense spending and social security, or conflicts between conservative and liberal political philosophies. But these are surface issues. The deeper issues are first, what values will we live by—absolute truth, the Holy Word of God, *or* the arbitrary, relative whims of the humanist elite; and second, who will set the moral agenda—the church *or* the bureaucratic social planners and vested economic interests of secular society?

America's moral leadership is up for grabs—and that is where you and I come in. The outcome of today's revolution will be determined by how we respond to the cries of our people for moral direction and vision.

Recent government budget

cutbacks put the challenge squarely before us. For 50 years, politicians have led us to believe that government could provide answers to all social ills. Their recipe was simple: enact a law, add at least one government agency, pour in money, and stir continuously.

But the ever-spiraling deficit and threat of grave economic consequences shatter that myth. We are learning that there are limits to what we once thought was the endless abundance of the American economy. So government deficits must be curbed, lest they continue to fuel morally indefensible, double-digit inflation.

But the resulting cutbacks hurt those most dependent on government aid, that is, the poor. If inflation is a moral issue, so too is society's concern for its disadvantaged and oppressed. We Christians know from the Old Testament prophets that a people who would sell the poor for a pair of shoes stand in fearsome judgment of Almighty God.

So the government's budget crisis raises a moral dilemma for our society and a spiritual issue for the church. How we respond will say much for the kind of people we are and hope to be; that's why I consider the budget crunch "Round One" in the battle for America's moral leadership.

The church faced one of its first tests in New York City several years ago, when 36,000 homeless men and women were wandering the city's streets at night. Mayor Edward Koch appealed to religious leaders for help: if each one of New York's 3,500 churches would care for just 10 homeless people, a desperate human problem could be quickly solved—and without huge government expense.

The *New York Times* reported the religious leaders' response. One Protestant representative was concerned about protocol: "The mayor never mentioned this to me. . . .

Nobody in his office called to apprise me of this." A Catholic spokesman sidestepped. A Jewish leader explained that many of the synagogues would not have money for increased heating bills.

The *Times* concluded: the church leaders would need more time to study the mayor's proposal. There was a disturbing silence from evangelicals.

One can almost imagine how it might sound on that day promised in Matthew 25 when our Lord says, "I was a stranger, and you did not invite Me in" (v. 43).

And the religious leaders will respond, "But, Lord, You didn't give us time to study the proposal."

I don't mean to belittle our brothers in New York; the issue is complicated and government cannot immediately transfer to the church full responsibility for the needy. But the sorry response should make us ask ourselves some tough questions. Have we become so caught up in doing our own thing, putting on massive television extravaganzas and organizing vast publishing and parachurch empires that we have lost sight of our biblical mission?

Church bureaucracies can become as bogged down as government bureaucracies, so wrapped up in writing pious statements of faith and issuing press releases that they forget their reason for existence: to proclaim the Good News and obey the clear commands of the Scriptures. Of course, the Bible requires justice and righteousness from government, but it also demands that *we* care about our neighbors, clothe the naked, feed the hungry, and visit the sick and those in prison. That's *us* our Lord is talking to, and we don't discharge that obligation by paying our taxes or dropping dimes in charity boxes. We discharge it by *doing* the Word of God.

Amazing things happen when we do exercise our biblical duty. Some time ago we took six convicts out of the federal prison in Florida and brought them to Atlanta, where each one was assigned to the home of a Prison Fellowship volunteer. Each morning the six convened for several hours of Bible study, then converged on the homes of two widows in a deteriorating section of the city. For two weeks they insulated, weather-stripped, caulked, sealed, and painted.

It was all part of a model project demonstrating that nonviolent criminals can do something better than vegetate in a prison cell at a cost to taxpayers of $17,000 per year. Without red tape and delays a project valued at $21,000 was completed at no cost to the public. It also proved that people getting busy helping other people can do the job faster and cheaper than cumbersome bureaucracies.

But Atlanta also gave us lessons of far greater significance. I visited one of the widows, Roxie Vaughn, 83 years old and blind. When we first told

Roxie her home was to be restored, she was elated. Then we told her six prisoners were going to do it and Roxie turned ashen. You see, she had had some personal experience with crime—her house had been broken into four times in the prior two years. She had lived in constant fear.

Well, by the third day those prisoners had worked around Roxie's home, she had them in for cookies and milk. The next afternoon television cameras caught a picture of Roxie sitting at her organ playing "Amazing Grace" with those six prisoners around her singing.

I spoke at the service at the end of the project. The widows were there. So were the volunteer families, who had hosted the inmates. None of them wanted to see their guests leave. The children were hugging the prisoners; the volunteers were hugging the widows. That dark, musty inner-city sanctuary that hadn't been filled in 40 years was jammed full of

Christians from all over Atlanta—
black and white, rich and poor—in the
most exciting and joyous worship
imaginable. We were witnessing the
incredible power of the Gospel to
heal prejudices, to deliver people from
fear, and to reconcile us to one
another.

Our 20th-century technology has
brought clinical impersonalization:
machines solve all problems;
television reduces us all to spectators
as life appears in a condensed version
from 6:00 to 7:00 each evening, in
living color. And the by-product of
modern technocracy is the loss of our
sense of caring and awareness of one
another. But if we Christians get out of
our pews, seek justice, do the Word
of God, and lift up Christ, we will see
that sense of community restored.

Think what this can mean for
evangelism. The world perceives us as
pious and self-centered in our
protected sanctuaries and multimillion-
dollar church complexes—but that is

simply not where most of the sick, hurting, and hungry people are, so they never hear our message. But imagine what would happen if the poor and needy could see us where *they* live, as we meet them at their point of need.

And, if we heed that call, we will be reasserting a proud heritage of the evangelical church. In the 19th century, evangelicals were at the forefront of the most significant social reforms in Western society: enacting child labor laws; ending abuses in the coal mines; establishing public education and public hospitals; and abolishing slavery.

"Round One" in the contest for America's moral leadership is still going on; whether the church is willing and able to step up to its biblical responsibility is still to be decided. It may be the greatest question we face. For if we fail even the simple test of responding to human needs in our own community, what possible claim will we have to assume a role of genuine

moral leadership in society? We dare
not fail.

A Different Kingdom

We are called to live and work and
serve in this world, but to give our total
allegiance to an entirely different
kingdom, what the Apostle Peter called
the "holy nation."

"You are a chosen race, a royal
priesthood, a holy nation, a people for
God's own possession, that you may
proclaim the excellencies of Him who
has called you out of darkness into
His marvelous light" (1 Peter 2:9).
Peter chose the very words Yahweh
used in speaking to Moses on Mount
Sinai, when He called His chosen
people—the Jews—to be a "holy
nation."

Ironic, isn't it, that Peter, the most
Jewish of the disciples, the one whom
God had to hit over the head three
times to get him to bring the Good

News to the Gentiles, the one who argued vehemently with Paul that Gentile believers must first become Jews, would be the one to use the term "holy nation," applying what had been the description of the Jews to *all* believers.

But Peter understood that the "holy nation" was not just another description of the church, but a real nation instituted and bound together by the Holy Creator of heaven and earth, at whose sovereign pleasure all the kingdoms of man are allowed to exist. To understand that we are members of the holy nation should evoke our deepest reverence.

But we live in an age in which the church seems to be beating a steady retreat in the face of the advancing forces of secular culture. And if we are honest, we must admit there's more of the world in the church than there is the church in the world.

So it has never been more important—or indeed, more difficult—

for American Christians to understand the difference between the holy nation and the nation-state. We must take our stand; let's consider what our holy citizenship means:

First, we must recognize that our eternal citizenship is in the kingdom of God. We are but sojourners in this nation, beloved though it is. We are clearly commanded by our Lord to seek *first* the kingdom of God (Matthew 6:33).

Many of us are frustrated by apostasy and declining morality in America today. It is evident on all sides: increasing abortion rates, family breakup, rampant pornography, deviant sexual practices accepted simply as alternative lifestyles, and—an issue especially painful to me—soaring crime rates. And so Christians today gather their skirts about them and yearn for the good ol' days of moral absolutes, when young people prayed in schools, parents retained authority over their children, folks loved their country, and life was so much simpler.

Many of our brethren have decided it's time to get involved; the most dramatic change in the American religious scene in recent years has been the emergence of fundamentalist churches into the political arena. Notoriously separatist in the past, concerned primarily with protecting their own piety against the contaminating influences of the outside, those churches are now the vanguard of a Christian crusade to restore morality to America.

Indeed, the decay of American culture demands our involvement. We believe there must be a Christian influence in every facet of society. Christians must participate, vote, work from within and without to see that government is an instrument of social justice.

But too there are grave pitfalls of failing to make clear the distinction between the holy nation and the nation-state. Christian moral and political movements, undertaken beneath the banner of simplistic God and country clichés, run this risk. Let me explain:

- First, no matter how well-motivated they are, some so-called Christian movements use God to sanctify the political prejudices of their adherents. And politicians are often willing partners in the process; I can testify from personal experience that politicians are not above using religious movements to their own advantage. The danger is that whenever we tie the Gospel to the political fortunes of any man or party, it is the Gospel that is made hostage and the Gospel that suffers.

- Second, Christian political movements can become exclusive. No one agenda can fit all moral situations.

Let us never limit God. He may burden you with one particular cause. He may burden me with another. In fact, I suspect that He assigns burdens and responsibilities throughout His kingdom; what might be on my agenda will not necessarily fit another equally dedicated Christian's agenda. The only absolute agenda is the uncompromising standard of righteousness and justice which Almighty God has woven through every page of His Holy Word.

- Third, in our passion to scrub America clean of its most obvious vices—homosexuality, abortion, pornography, etc.—we narrow the scope of Christian concern. And, by our silence, we implicitly embrace those things not on our hit list, aligning ourselves with the subtle sins of privilege, power, conspicuous affluence. We do it in a way our Lord very pointedly eschewed.

The American church, fairly or unfairly, is perceived as a white, Anglo-Saxon, upper-middle-class phenomenon. The same folks who dine at the country club on Saturday evenings, rub shoulders on padded pews at their gilded churches on Sunday mornings. The danger is that we become so identified with an affluent American lifestyle, that people who can't or won't accept the values of that culture, can't or won't accept the Gospel of Christ.

Time after time I find that men and women in the prisons of America want nothing to do with the church or with Christianity. They cannot relate to our lavish buildings and stained-glass windows because they see the church as a manifestation of the culture which has rejected them and holds them prisoner. But I see those same people come alive when I talk about Jesus the prisoner, the outcast who was followed by a dirty dozen, the One who was laid in a borrowed manger, rode on a borrowed donkey, was arrested, hung on a cross between two thieves, and then buried in a borrowed tomb. They can understand and identify with the Jesus of the

Scriptures, not with a Christ who appears to have just stepped out of a Brooks Brothers catalog.

The longer I'm a Christian, the more I realize that the vague deity of American civil religion is a heretical rejection of the Christ of Holy Scripture. So don't confuse your loyalties—never assume the will of the majority and the will of God are synonymous. They may be different—and frequently are.

The Christian is committed to work for justice and righteousness, to bring the Gospel of Christ to bear in all areas of life to make a difference in society. But we do it by the integrity of our witness, not by resorting to quick, simplistic clichés.

Brotherhood and Worship

Second, as citizens of the holy nation, we necessarily and automatically become part of a community beyond ourselves. Many Christians think of conversion as personal and private. But being converted is not just being separated—or "saved"—from one's sinful past; it is being joined to a holy God and His people. That is the very essence of the convenant.

That sounds simple, but living it is not. Ours is a conspicuously egocentric era. Books like *Looking Out for Number One* and *Winning through Intimidation* have been the bestsellers of the past decade. Another evidence of our self-absorption has become a booming industry: video games. It's a form of electronic solitaire, as if 230 million people had so lost their capacity to relate to one another that they are more comfortable staring at Pac-Man chewing up his opponents than they are looking at each other.

We Christians must be different, prepared to live not by the self-aggrandizing rules of this culture, but by that commandment which tells us to bear one another's burdens and to lay down our lives for one another. Let me illustrate:

- Next to my conversion, the most powerful spiritual experience of my life was when, in prison, I learned that a member of my prayer group, who happened then to be the eighth-ranking Republican in the House of Representatives, now the former governor of Minnesota, had asked the President if he could serve my remaining sentence in my place so I could be with my wife and kids, who were experiencing serious problems. *That is citizenship in the holy nation.*

- At a White House meeting in 1982, I was thrilled when President Reagan referred to Agape House, a project in Jefferson City, Missouri, as an illustration of what Christian groups should be doing. Agape House started a few years ago when volunteers in our ministry and concerned citizens in the community discovered that wives traveling from St. Louis and Kansas City to visit their husbands in the state penitentiary had no place to stay, and often slept in cars or in parks. The group bought an old house and renovated it as a guest home where inmates' families could get food, lodging, and Christian love. *That is citizenship in the holy nation.*

- A couple in Denver recently mortgaged their home to get bail money for an inmate they had been ministering to. *That's citizenship in the holy nation.*

Since we are part of a corporate body, we bear corporate responsibility for what happens around us. All too often we Christians act as if we secretly delight in the moral pollution around us; the more depraved the world is, the more righteous we feel by comparison.

That can be very dangerous. Remember Nehemiah: before he undertook the extraordinary task of rebuilding the walls of Jerusalem, he prayed that God would forgive him his sins . . . *and the sins of his fathers* (1:6). When God's judgment comes on a people it comes upon the just as well as the unjust.

Doctors in a clinic in Chicago are so overworked they cannot take time between abortions to fill out the forms for payment, so they make hash marks on their bloodstained smocks, casually totaling them up at the end of each day. We recoil in horror, relieved that we are not part of such a desecration of God's creation. But of course we are—inescapably so. We of the holy nation within the nation-state need to be a deeply repentant people whose hearts are contrite and break over the practices of our culture that break the heart of God.

Third, as members of the holy nation, we worship the unseen God, who through His Son dwells in each of us. We are to respect and follow those in whom God reposes spiritual authority, but we must remember that ours is a jealous Sovereign. The first four of the Ten Commandments deal not with our sins against our fellowman but with the requirements of exclusive worship and reverence for our Creator God.

Americans have come to worship fame for fame's sake. To be the object of adulation in America, one needs only to appear frequently enough on television to be generally recognized; it has nothing to do with why the person is famous. As British journalist Henry Fairlie said, "We say correctly of some people that they idolize success, but our societies as a whole also worship it, and again the celebrity is a symbol. We do not applaud his talents, even if he should have any; we applaud his success."

Just look at the utterly idolatrous worship of Elvis Presley. A $500,000 collection of Presley artifacts toured the country several years ago, attracting as many as 200,000 viewers at each stop. The display manager, who spent $1,000 for one of the most popular items—a pair of Presley's underpants—told reporters, "I almost didn't buy them . . . but the women just went nuts over them, wanted their pictures taken with them." Millions of Americans fanatically worship the memory of this dead man who would hole up for months eating compulsively, ogling porno films, who was so stoned most of the time that he couldn't control his bowels during the night. That we have so extolled this pathetic man says more about us than Presley. As Shakespeare wrote in *Macbeth,* "Fair is foul and foul is fair." Similarly, the Bible says, "Woe to those who call evil good, and good evil" (Isaiah 5:20) and to those "whose god is their appetite, and whose glory is in their shame" (Philippians 3:19).

What is it about us that causes us to withhold from God the reverence we lavish on human idols? Over and over in the White House, I met people who would fiercely complain about a policy and demand an audience with the President. But the roaring lions I escorted from the waiting room became meek lambs in the Oval Office. I saw more awe in that one room than I have seen in the sanctuaries of all our churches combined.

But that is the secular world, you say. Well, that same attitude has captured much of the Christian world. Instead of the pelvis-grinding rendition of "Hound Dog," we Christians have substituted Pepsodent smiles, spray-dried hair, and syrupy baritones, all slickly directed before expensive video cameras. But just because we're electronically as good as Johnny Carson doesn't mean that we are penetrating the world with the convicting message of Christ.

The Word and Holy Living

Fourth, as citizens of the holy nation, we take our stand not on the shifting sands of secular relativism but on the holy and inerrant Word of God. Decisions in the world are made on the basis of expedience and changing sociological factors. But the Word is unchanging, immutable, and without it we Christians have nothing.

Taking our stand on biblical truth can be our only defense against our culture's penchant to reduce all issues to simplistic suppositions and glib answers. We impatiently expect to get solutions to the most profound ambiguities of life the same way we drive up to the fast-food counter: one double burger, chocolate shake, and an order of fries. We are faddists. Just look at the rash of new diets and instant physical-conditioning courses which week after week dominate our bestseller lists.

The problem is, that "easy-answer"

mentality is invading the Christian church: we want scorecards by which we can instantly rate our politicians, new catchy acronyms for salvation, time-saving techniques for discipleship. But formulas don't convert people; slick slogans and cute phrases are no substitute for hard spiritual truth.

In our well-intentioned effort to reach unsaved masses, we often make the Gospel message itself sound easy, unthreatening, a painless answer to all life's ills. We portray a loving God who forgives all and asks nothing in return. Now, that may tickle the ears of this pleasure-seeking generation, but it is nothing less than heresy.

As citizens in the holy nation, we must challenge presuppositions—not only of society as a whole but of the evangelical subculture as well. The Gospel of Jesus Christ must be the bad news of the conviction of sin before it can be the Good News of redemption. The truth is revealed in

God's Holy Word; life can be lived
only in absolute and disciplined
submission to its authority.

Fifth, we are commanded not only
to seek first the kingdom of God—don't
stop there—but His righteousness as
well.

Righteousness or holy living is
often seen by Christians as maintaining
chaste sexual standards, tithing,
faithful church attendance, being
friendly to those around us. Well,
those are indeed Christian responsibilities, but only the beginning
of holy living.

And many believers categorize
their refraining from alcohol, tobacco,
cards, and dancing as holy living.
Though God may call you to that type
of witness, it is only skimming the
surface at best. That is piety. And we
must never, never confuse piety with
righteousness.

Righteousness was defined by
Yahweh at Mount Sinai and interpreted
by the fiery words of His prophets

from Isaiah to Amos to Habakkuk and, ultimately, by the life of His Son, Jesus. God's definition of righteousness is based on justice for all people, especially the unfortunate: you shall not sell the poor for a pair of shoes, nor take away the coat of a man who borrows from you; you shall pay your employees a just wage; you shall care for widows and orphans; you shall hate evil and do good. "Remodel your courts into true halls of justice," thundered the Prophet Amos (see Amos 5:15). "Let justice roll down like waters and righteousness like an ever-flowing stream" (v. 24). That's God's standard of righteousness and holy living.

After 10 years in a Soviet gulag, Alexander Solzhenitsyn wrote, "Bless you, prison, for having been in my life." For it was there he learned that "the meaning of earthly existence lies, not as we have grown used to thinking, in prospering, but in the development of the soul." I too can

say, "Bless you, prison," for it was
there that I learned to see justice in the
way that Amos and Micah and
Jeremiah and Isaiah saw it, the way it is
to be in the holy nation.

When I was in law and politics, I
believed justice was determined by a
majority vote, 50 percent plus 1.
Justice was simply the law, which I
tried to influence, often on behalf of
very affluent clients. In the White
House I saw justice as the sum of
rules and policies which I tried to
shape, often on behalf of those
people whose influence—or campaign
contribution—was significant
enough to get them past the White
House gates and into my office.

Then too I had grown up in the
insecurity of the Depression,
believing deeply in the work ethic;
justice was also protecting
individuals' earnings and keeping the
government from interfering with
their rights.

Finally, of course, justice was the

instrument for punishing and removing from society those who refused—or were unable—to live by the rules that people like myself made.

But from a prison cell I saw men condemned to waste away for long years—for what seemed like trivial offenses. Like most people, I had thought prisons were populated by violent, dangerous criminals. What a shock to find that the man in the bunk next to me was a former bank vice-president who battled the government for nine years over $3,000 of tax evasion. For a first offense, he received a three-year sentence. I found young men who couldn't afford lawyers like I had been; in fact, they couldn't afford any lawyer at all. I found others who were sentenced without knowing why—or for how long. It was in a prison cell that I came to understand why God makes special demands on His people to care for the oppressed, sick, suffering, and needy.

Justice is not achieved in God's eyes until a society is as concerned with the rights and dignity of the man in a prison cell as it is with the man in the executive suite. If we're honest, I suspect we will agree that we're as far away from that standard today as the holy nation was in the time of Amos. But that standard is what you and I must work for.

Sixth, we must be prepared as citizens of the holy nation to take our stand in faithful obedience to our Lord, to make a difference with our lives. That will probably mean standing against the culture in "a bold and majestic witness to the holy commandments of God," as Carl Henry has put it. That does not just mean contributing or paying dues to some moralistic crusade. It means standing in the gap, if need be, by yourself.

The late Francis Schaeffer once wrote and told me of meeting believers in various walks of life whose Christian faith was making absolutely no difference in their vocations. He concluded, "We talk a lot about the need of having true Christians getting into the media, the chaplaincy, etc. . . . but there is no use for our people getting into the media or the chaplaincy or anything else unless they are willing for confrontation when necessary, even when it is costly to their careers."

Exactly right. Let me give you one illustration—there are many—of what it can mean for a Christian to take his stand against the culture.

In 1977 Harry Fred Palmer, a Vietnam veteran, was arrested in Elkhart, Indiana for burglary; while in jail awaiting trial he accepted Christ. His offense carried a mandatory minimum sentence of 10 years—although that law, acknowledged as arbitrary by the legislature, had been changed 18 days after Palmer's arrest.

The judge assigned to the case, William Bontrager, had himself been converted to Christ recently. He reviewed the facts, concluded the 10-year minimum statute unconstitutional, and sentenced Palmer to one year in prison with the provision he thereafter make restitution to those he had robbed, and perform community service.

Palmer did just that. He served his year, a model prisoner, active in Prison Fellowship programs. After his release he began paying back his victims and was reunited with his wife and family. The case was a model of justice, restitution, and restoration.

But the Indiana Supreme Court swung into action, claiming that Bontrager's suspension of the mandatory sentence was unconstitutional. Palmer should serve the remaining nine years of his automatic sentence, they said, even though the law requiring it was no longer in existence. They ordered Bontrager to send him back to jail.

For Bontrager, the court's order was clearly a case of choosing to obey the law of man or the law of God. He had been reading the Old Testament prophets; God's demands for justice and righteousness had seared his conscience. He knew the Supreme Court's order would serve neither, merely a technicality of the law.

So he disqualified himself, turning the case over to another judge. A nightmarish sequence of events followed. The court slammed Palmer back behind bars, declared Bontrager in contempt, fined him $500, and sentenced him to 30 days in prison. Though that sentence was suspended, the court began proceedings to remove him from the bench. Rather than allow his own struggle to endanger Palmer's chance for appeals, Judge Bontrager resigned.

It was not a painless decision. He gave up a comfortable salary, the judgeship he had worked all his life to attain, and the security of community respect. But Judge Bontrager's spiritual discernment was keen—he knew to send a man back to prison for a debt he had already paid was at odds with the standard of justice of the holy God he served. So he had to take his stand—whatever the cost.

Though your arena may not be the courtroom, I guarantee you will have many opportunities, small and large, to take your stand. If not, you need to question your own commitment. Conformity is the high priest of American culture, and has infiltrated the holy nation. So it is not easy, but I beseech you, *dare to be different.* Dare to live as a citizen of the holy nation.

Time for Action

Seventh, and finally, citizens of the holy nation must participate in the human drama. Much of the church today has withdrawn, seeking refuge on the high ground. Our multimillion-dollar church complexes are as remote and protected as walled medieval fortresses, protected from the swirling waters where most of the sick, hungry, and hurting people are. So those in need cannot identify with us and will consequently never hear our message. But imagine what would happen if they see us where they live, as we meet them at their point of need.

Jacques Ellul wrote that until we have "really understood the actual plight of our contemporaries and we have heard their cry of anguish, until we have shared their suffering both physical and spiritual, and their despair and desolation, then we shall be able to proclaim the Word of God, but not until then." The Apostle Paul called it the fellowship of suffering (Philippians 3:10). It is a spiritual mystery—suffering with others draws us closer to our Christ who suffered for us.

Being in prison has given me this insight. For the most meaningful communions I have had with my Lord have not been in the great cathedrals of the world I've been privileged to preach in, nor in the parliaments where I have spoken, nor in the most influential gatherings of Christian leaders. They have been instead on my knees on the grimy, concrete floor of a rotten prison cell with my hand on the shoulder of a tough convict who sobs with joy as we meet Another who was in prison, executed, and rose from a tomb for us—His name is Jesus.

My friends, take your posts. You have been called out by the most high and holy God to serve Him in the building of His holy nation. You are called not to be successful or to meet any of the other counterfeit standards of this world, but to be faithful and to be expended in the cause of serving the risen and returning Christ.